For Pam

Thank you for your patience and support.

And in loving memory of my own country greats

Joe Wofford and Halden Starr Bertholf.

⊢BB

Little, Brown and Company

Hachette Book Group USA
1271 Avenue of the Americas, New York, NY 10020
Visit our Web site at www.lb-kids.com

First Edition: April 2007

Library of Congress Cataloging-in-Publication Data

Bertholf, Bret.
  Long gone lonesome history of country music / Bret Bertholf.—1st ed.
    p. cm.
  ISBN-10 0-316-52393-3 (hardcover) ISBN-13 978-0-316-52393-6 (hardcover)
 1. Country music—History and criticism—Juvenile literature. I. Title.
ML3524.B46 2006
781.642'09—dc22   2005016036

10 9 8 7 6 5 4 3 2 1

TWP

Printed in Singapore

The illustrations for this book were done in colored pencil
and Caran d'Ache crayon on Canson pastel paper.
The text was set in T-26 Archetype, and the display type is Wanted.

the LONG GONE LONESOME HISTORY OF COUNTRY MUSIC

by BRET BERTHOLF

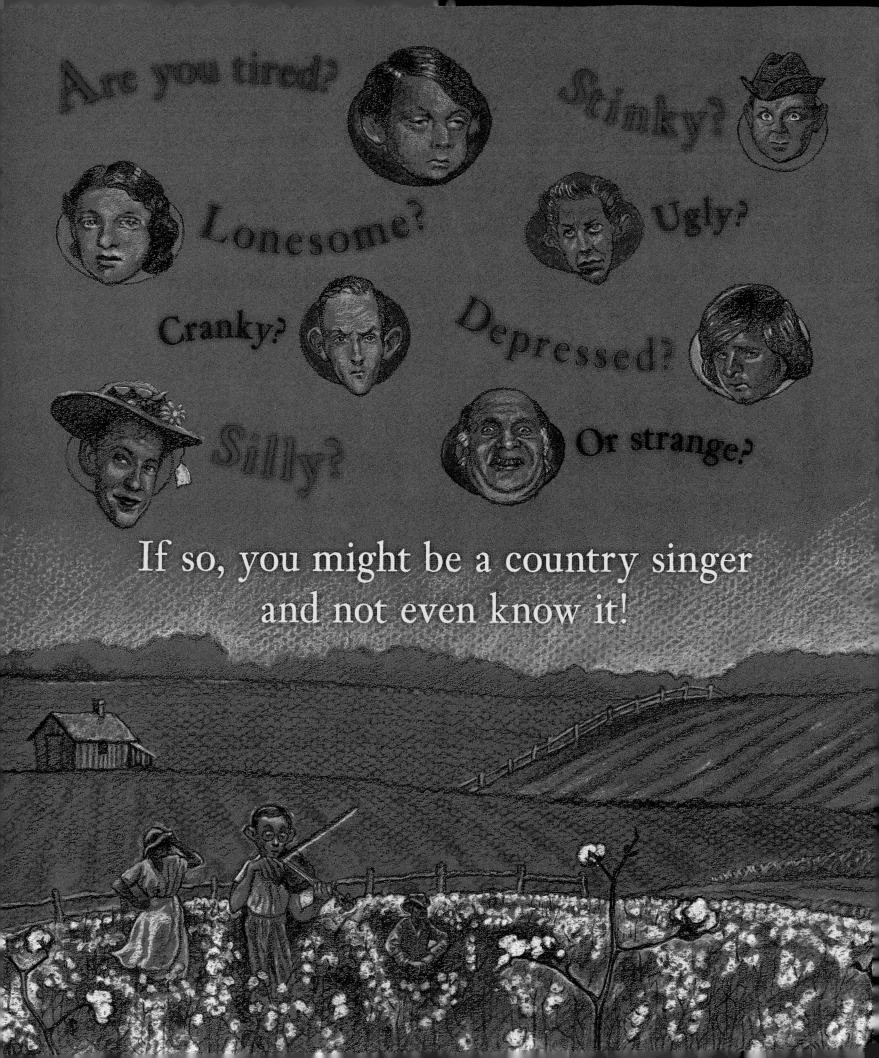

Are you tired? Stinky? Lonesome? Ugly? Cranky? Depressed? Silly? Or strange?

If so, you might be a country singer
and not even know it!

A lot of people wouldn't know, because there's a lot
to know about country music, and it's hard to remember
all of it.

You're not gonna believe this, but there was a time
before movies, before video games, before cars, when
America was a brand-new country. Back then, if you
didn't live in a city, and you wanted to hear some music,
you had to make it yourself.

Sure, sometimes you'd get to go over to a farmer's barn,
where folks would spread out the hay and dance all night,
but mostly you had to make do around the house or out
in the field.

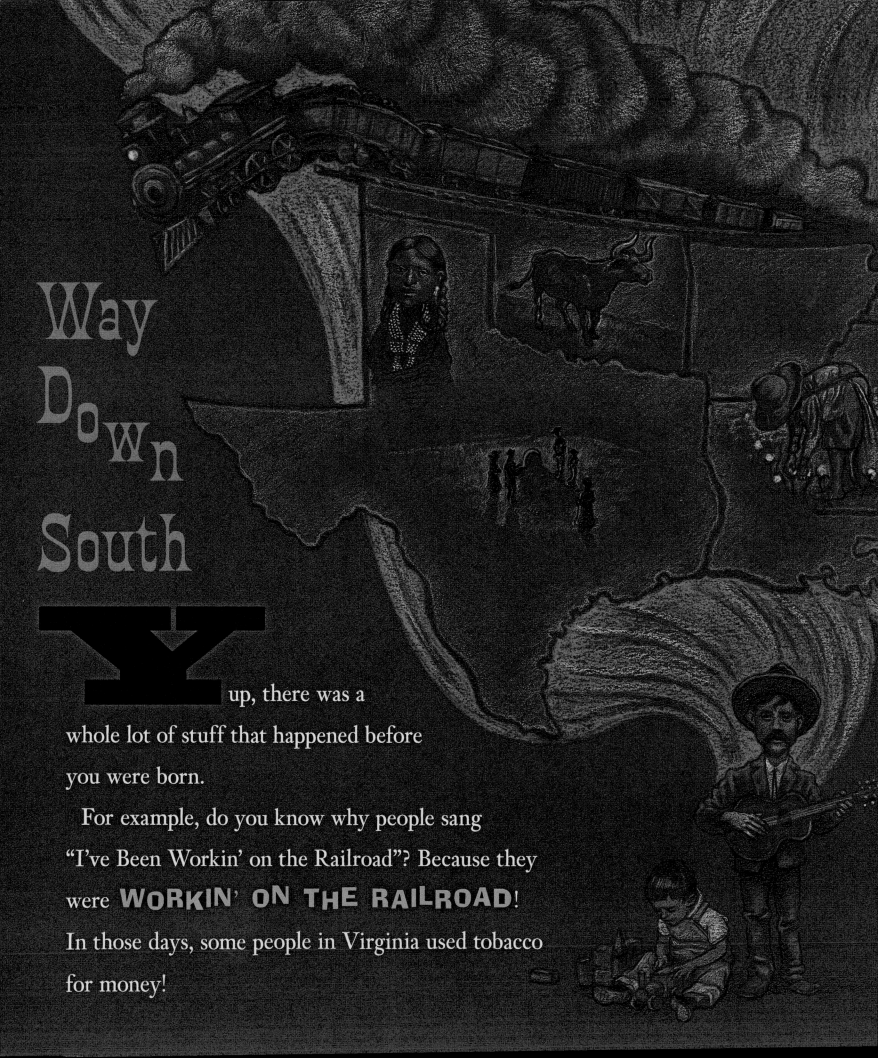

Way Down South

Yup, there was a whole lot of stuff that happened before you were born.

For example, do you know why people sang "I've Been Workin' on the Railroad"? Because they were **WORKIN' ON THE RAILROAD**! In those days, some people in Virginia used tobacco for money!

There wasn't much to play with, either. There were dolls made from corn husks, toy trains carved out of wood, and homemade puzzles. You could climb an oak tree, swim in a duck pond, or play with your hair. Or, you could make up a song about the things you did, like telling a story.

Country music is all about making up songs about what people did. And people did a lot. They fought in wars, built houses and railroads, got married, picked cotton, and died.

And some people got good at making things up.

COUNTRY INSTRUMENTS

Even if you don't have any money, you can find something in your home to make country music with. In the beginning, people even used **SPOONS**. Washboards were used for scrubbing clothes, but if you take a knife or a fork to one, it can become a rhythm instrument!

RADIO DAYS

mericans **LOVE** to invent things. Like the telephone and the record player and the cotton gin and cars.

After those things, do you know what the next big invention to come along was? The **RADIO**!

In just ten years, from 1917 to 1927, over 12 MILLION people owned radios. And if you have that many radios, you gotta have something for them to play.

In the 1920s the air crackled with broadcasts of music from those dances in barns. Can you guess what they called the shows? **BARN DANCES**! Are you surprised?

People danced in their living rooms, by the light of candles and oil lamps, laughing because they didn't have to go to a barn, and there was less chance of stepping in cow poo. And **NOBODY** likes stepping in cow poo. **NOBODY**!

EARLY RECORDS

Would you drive 25 miles in an old, bumpy Ford wagon, almost three hours each way, going over a mountain in Virginia, fixing **THREE** flat tires, and sweating in the hot August sun, just so you might record a song and maybe get paid $50?

In 1927, a whole slew of country folks did because men from New York record companies were driving around the south looking for music they could record and sell. Everyone who sang, yodeled, fiddled, or strummed wanted to try out: whole families in beat-up wagons, mothers with babies on their knees, friends and neighbors with ceramic jugs and store-bought accordions! They all thought it was an easier way to make money than farming or workin' on the railroad all the livelong day. And they were right!

My name is **Jimmie Rodgers**, and do you know what I did that made people sit up and listen to my records? I YODELED!

Yodeling may be a silly thing, but I did it really well. In the '20s and '30s everybody **LOVED** it, and it caught on quicker than tuberculosis, and spread just as fast. You could buy whole books on how to do it!

And that's how I became America's first country music star.

COUNTRY ALL-STAR

HOW TO YODEL!

First, pretend you're swallowing a monkey. Now, sing a high note and get your best friend to pinch your posterior. A healthy YELP will get you yodeling.

(Remember, once your voice breaks it'll stay broke.)

Don't Look?

YODELIN'
HALL O' FAME

Jimmie Rodgers
Where Yodels came from
Now do it louder! NO, louder than that! (You gotta scare some dogs.)
Patsy Montana
Don Walser

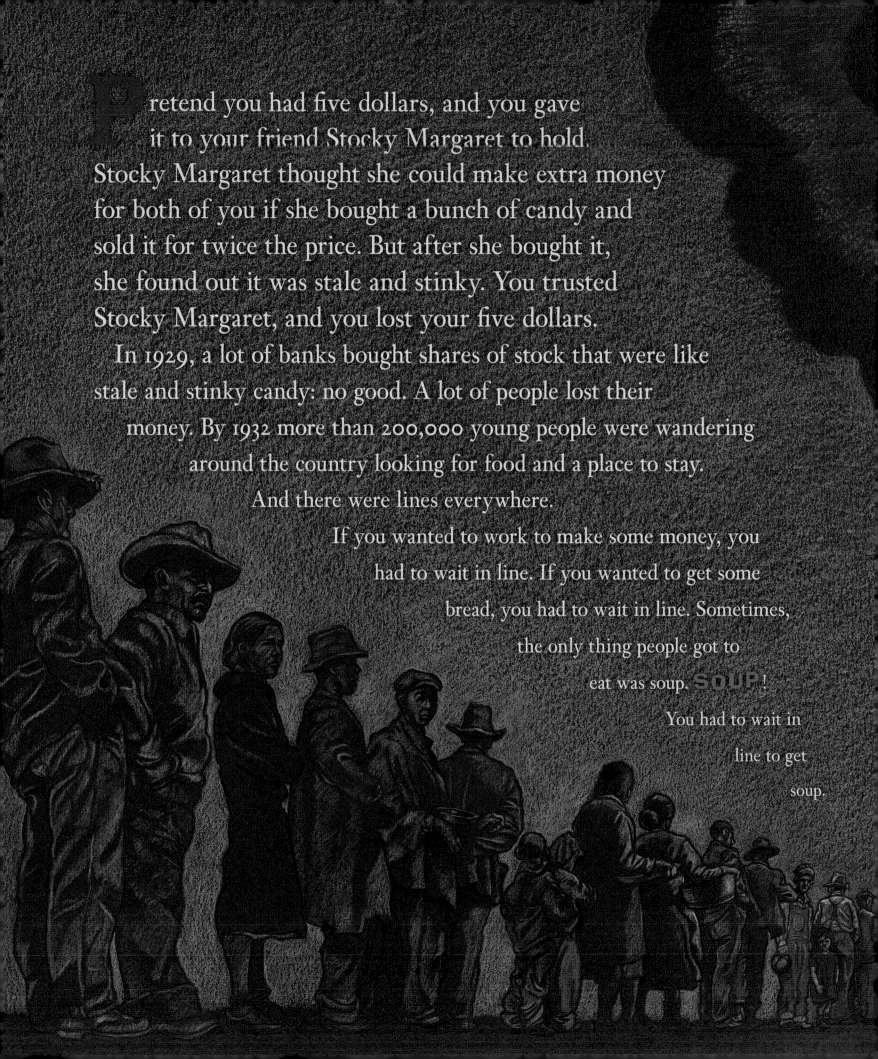

Pretend you had five dollars, and you gave
it to your friend Stocky Margaret to hold.
Stocky Margaret thought she could make extra money
for both of you if she bought a bunch of candy and
sold it for twice the price. But after she bought it,
she found out it was stale and stinky. You trusted
Stocky Margaret, and you lost your five dollars.

In 1929, a lot of banks bought shares of stock that were like
stale and stinky candy: no good. A lot of people lost their
money. By 1932 more than 200,000 young people were wandering
around the country looking for food and a place to stay.
And there were lines everywhere.
If you wanted to work to make some money, you
had to wait in line. If you wanted to get some
bread, you had to wait in line. Sometimes,
the only thing people got to
eat was soup. SOUP!
You had to wait in
line to get
soup.

Yes, sir, America in the 1930s was not always a nice place to be. For years there was little or no rain on the Great Plains, and storms of dust wiped away people's crops and land. Many farmers moved to California, looking for a better life. Kids as young as eight and nine worked in factories and on farms and never got to go to school. And sometimes, people were attacked just because of the color of their skin, or because they didn't have any money. It was like the world had a dark cloud hanging over it.

But people sang songs about these bad things, too, telling the world what they saw and how they felt. Sometimes, singing a song is like turning on a light during a scary movie.

GOSPEL ROOTS

Like I said, Americans like to invent things. Soon all kinds of people, from all kinds of backgrounds, were making up and mixing up songs. Sometimes they stole ideas from each other, and other times they were inspired by the same things.

For a lot of them, the church was the first place they ever heard music, and so church songs, hymns, and **GOSPEL MUSIC** became the pattern for the songs they made up.

SINGING

Tired of waiting in lines for everything, many Americans began moving west looking for better lives and jobs. And if you're gonna move west, where there are wide open spaces, and cows and horses, you'll want to be one thing:

A COWBOY!

COWBOYS

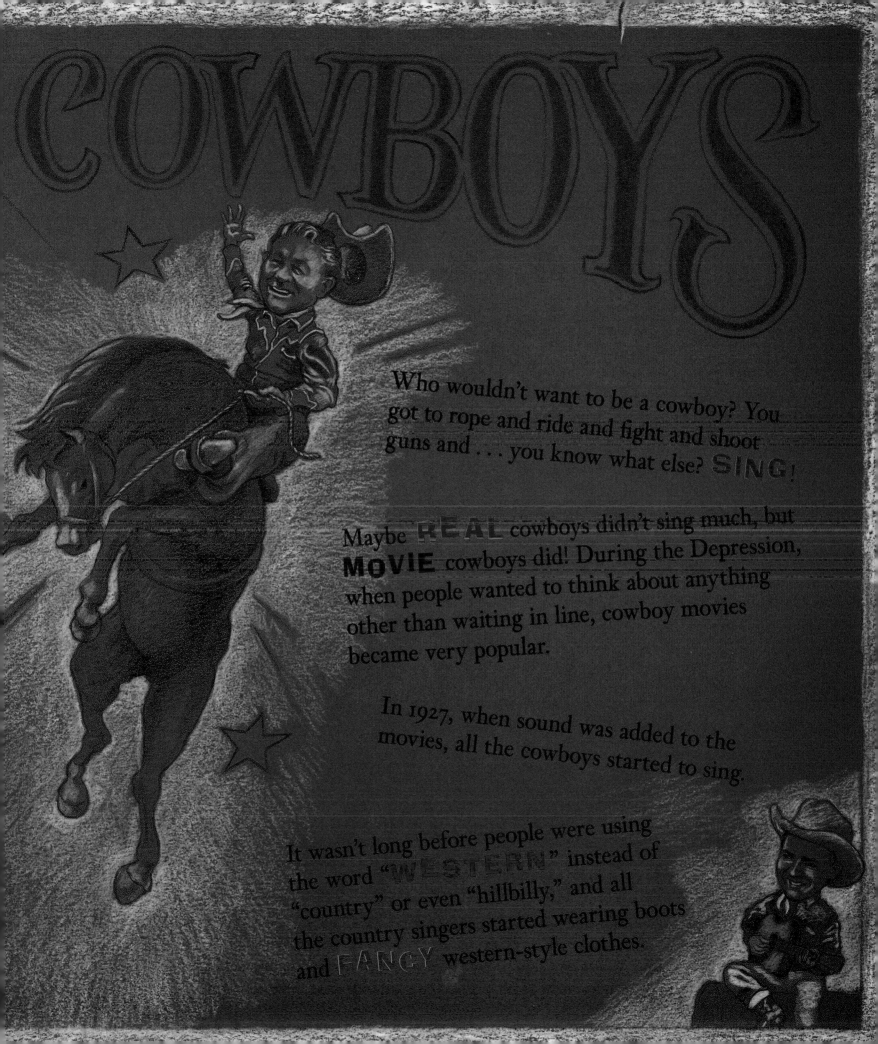

Who wouldn't want to be a cowboy? You got to rope and ride and fight and shoot guns and . . . you know what else? **SING**!

Maybe **REAL** cowboys didn't sing much, but **MOVIE** cowboys did! During the Depression, when people wanted to think about anything other than waiting in line, cowboy movies became very popular.

In 1927, when sound was added to the movies, all the cowboys started to sing.

It wasn't long before people were using the word "**WESTERN**" instead of "country" or even "hillbilly," and all the country singers started wearing boots and **FANCY** western-style clothes.

If you want to look "country," there are certain things you should wear. At first, if you were a **HILLBILLY** or a **HICK** or a **YOKEL**, it meant that you lived in the country and were ignorant or poor and had to make all your own clothes by hand.

But after the singing cowboy movies, wanted to look like a cowboy! Especially people who played country music.

My name is Nudie Cohn, and I made the **WILDEST**, most **COLORFUL**, **FLASHY**, rhinestone-studded, **GLOW-IN-THE-DARK** cowboy suits you'll ever see. I moved to America from Russia when I was eleven years old, in 1913. Then, when I was sixteen, I moved to California to try to be a boxer. That didn't work out too well, but with the help of singing cowboy Tex Williams, I started making **COWBOY CLOTHES** for the movies. Some of the clothes I made were so shiny you couldn't even look at 'em!

HILLBILLY JAZZ

Do you get the feeling that country music is about as MIXED UP as a bowl of jambalaya?

That's because IT IS! Remember when I told you that Americans love to invent things? JAZZ is one of those things.

J azz is an   kind of music that starts with a basic pattern of notes, but then you can make it up as you go along, like a game. Nowadays, there are all kinds of jazz, but when it first cropped up, people had never heard anything like it.

What did people do in the late 1930s to forget their troubles? They went to the movies, and they danced. What did they dance to? Jazz! There was even a country version of jazz.

In America's southwest, musicians heard jazz, German Polkas and waltzes, even Native-American and Mexican ranchera music. They snapped their fingers and mixed them all up together to make a new country sound: WESTERN SWING. Some people called it "hillbilly jazz," and it had people dancing all the way through World War II!

My name is **Bob Wills**, and I came from a town called Turkey, Texas. Way back in the burly early days of the 1920s, when I was a young man, you could hear a lot of different kinds of music. But I sure loved jazz and blues. One time I rode 50 miles on a horse just to see Bessie Smith, the famous blues singer, perform.

When I started playing on radio shows, a flour company paid me to sing songs and then talk about how good the flour was for making biscuits. My first band was called the Light Crust Dough Boys, the same name as the company! But after I got tired of eating biscuits, we started a new band called the Texas Playboys. We played all over the South and West, all the way out to California.

During World War II, I got kicked out of the army because I was too fat and too crabby for training. I just went back to the one thing I did best: leading a big band and shouting in the middle of the songs, like this:

"Come out mama, the hogs has got me,"

and

"shoot low sheriff, he's ridin' a Shetland!"

WORLD WAR II

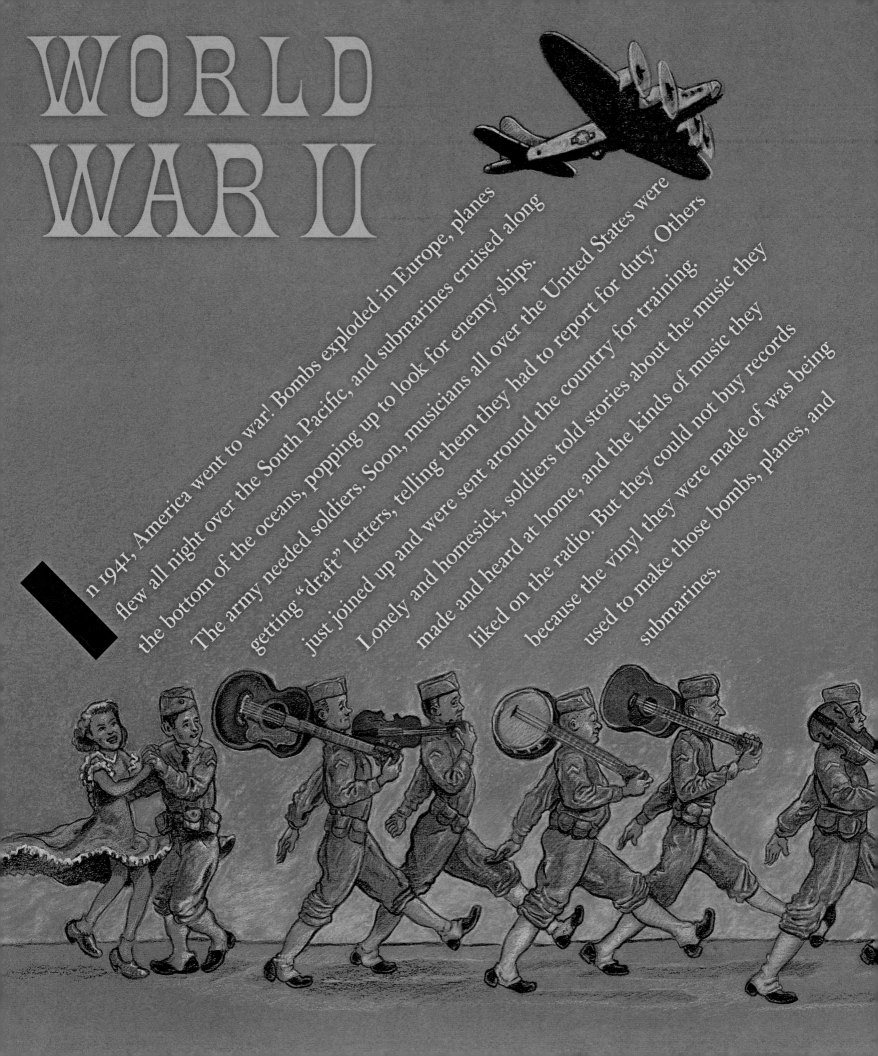

In 1941, America went to war! Bombs exploded in Europe, planes flew all night over the South Pacific, and submarines cruised along the bottom of the oceans, popping up to look for enemy ships. The army needed soldiers. Soon, musicians all over the United States were getting "draft" letters, telling them they had to report for duty. Others just joined up and were sent around the country for training. Lonely and homesick, soldiers told stories about the music they made and heard at home, and the kinds of music they liked on the radio. But they could not buy records because the vinyl they were made of was being used to make those bombs, planes, and submarines.

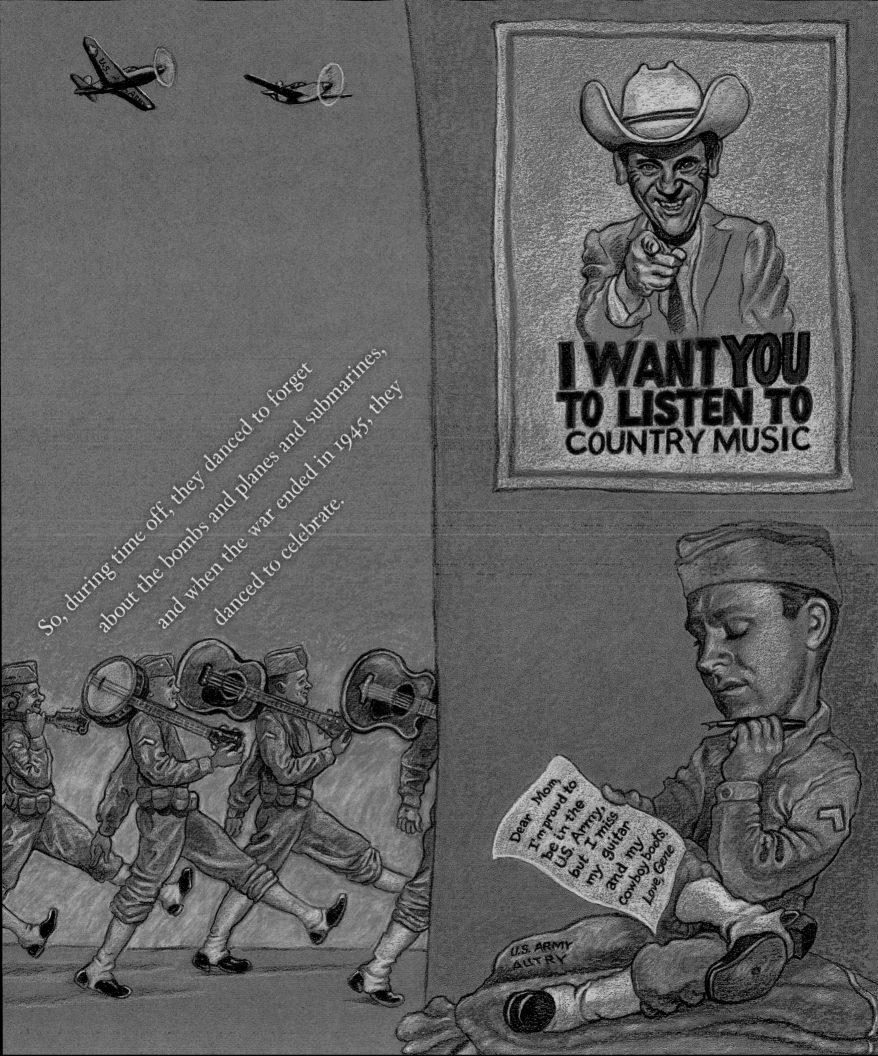

So, during time off, they danced to forget about the bombs and planes and submarines, and when the war ended in 1945, they danced to celebrate.

COUNTRY PETS

If you sing country music, or just live in the country, these are the pets for YOU!

Hound Dog
(but remember, these squawk all the time...)

Mean-Eyed Cat
(funny to look at, not very nice.)

HAWG
(good pets, but sometimes they talk to spiders...)

HORSE
(best for singing cowboys)

Squeezal
(very weird)

VARMINTS
(I don't know what these are...)

Snakes
(quiet & fun, if you can handle them!)

Chicken
(good but Vain...)

COUNTRY VEE-HICKLES

It's hard to say what the best way to get around in the country might be, but if you sing country music, consider these options:

The fanciest car in country music!

Easy to rhyme with.

"JALOPY"

what most people
end up driving

TOUR BUS
(if you're famous)

HAND CAR
(a hard way
to get to work)

When the soldiers came home, they had to find jobs, and many people looked around the country for work. Isn't it funny how, in America, we have places to go to do different things? If you want to make movies, you go to Hollywood. If you want to race cars, you go to Indianapolis. And if you want to make country music, you go to Nashville, Tennessee.

Since Nashville is **SMACK DAB** in the center of the south, it was easy for all the new singers to get there. Plus, it had the GRAND OLE OPRY, which had the biggest, most popular BARN DANCE of them all. Record companies had to build huge new studios just to record all the new people in town.

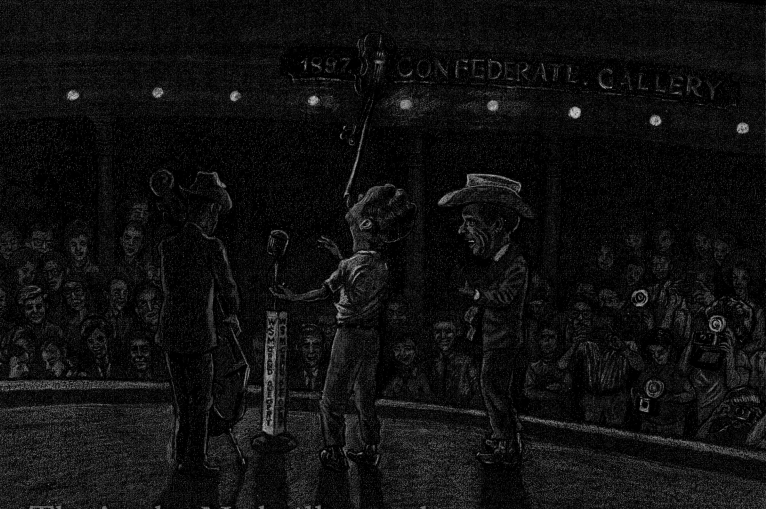

That's why Nashville got the name

"MUSIC CITY."

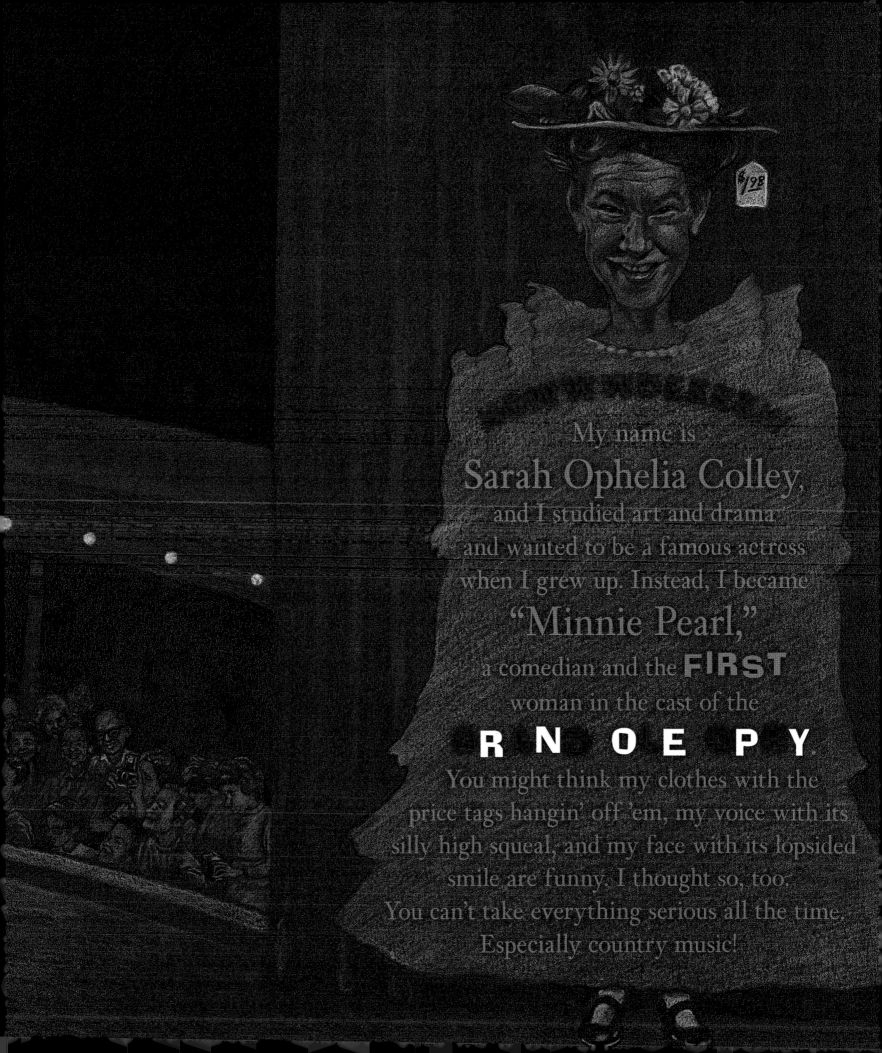

My name is
Sarah Ophelia Colley,
and I studied art and drama
and wanted to be a famous actress
when I grew up. Instead, I became
"Minnie Pearl,"
a comedian and the **FIRST**
woman in the cast of the
R N O E P Y.
You might think my clothes with the
price tags hangin' off 'em, my voice with its
silly high squeal, and my face with its lopsided
smile are funny. I thought so, too.
You can't take everything serious all the time.
Especially country music!

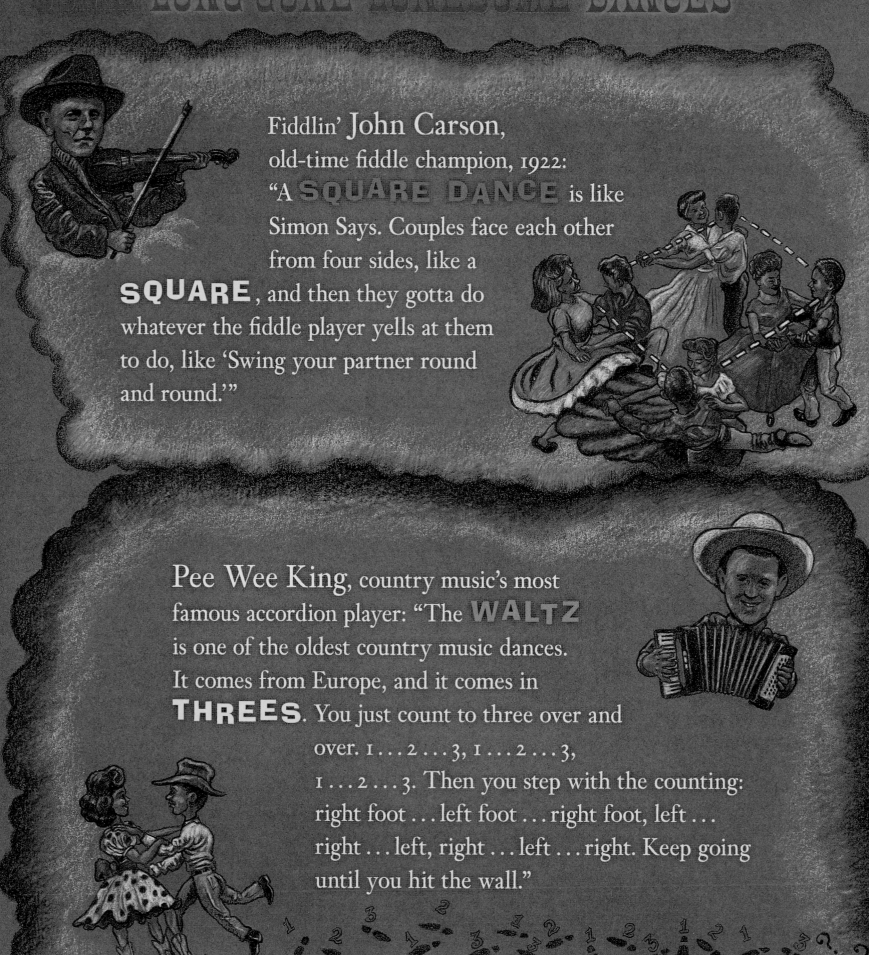

Fiddlin' John Carson, old-time fiddle champion, 1922: "A **SQUARE DANCE** is like Simon Says. Couples face each other from four sides, like a **SQUARE**, and then they gotta do whatever the fiddle player yells at them to do, like 'Swing your partner round and round.'"

Pee Wee King, country music's most famous accordion player: "The **WALTZ** is one of the oldest country music dances. It comes from Europe, and it comes in **THREES**. You just count to three over and over. 1 . . . 2 . . . 3, 1 . . . 2 . . . 3, 1 . . . 2 . . . 3. Then you step with the counting: right foot . . . left foot . . . right foot, left . . . right . . . left, right . . . left . . . right. Keep going until you hit the wall."

Rose Maddox, the "Queen of Country Swing": "SWING dancing started in New York City during the Depression, but after World War II, returning GIs brought it to the country. It's the most dangerous dancing there is because people flip and slide and jump and swing around each other like acrobats in the circus!"

Billy Ray Cyrus, a singer with an Achy Breaky Heart: "If you wanna LINE DANCE, you need at least two friends. First, you gotta line up. Then, everybody does the same thing. Even if you just step forward and back, make sure you stay in line. It's kinda like marching, and it's not as easy as it looks."

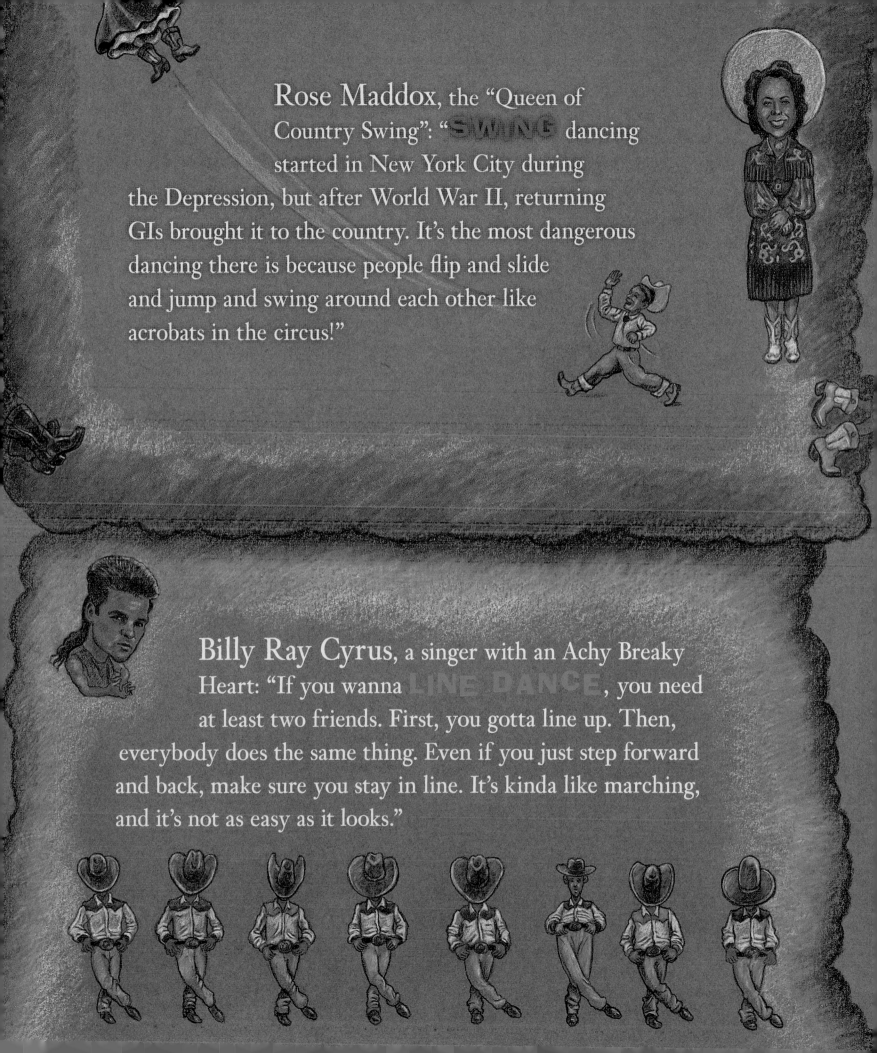

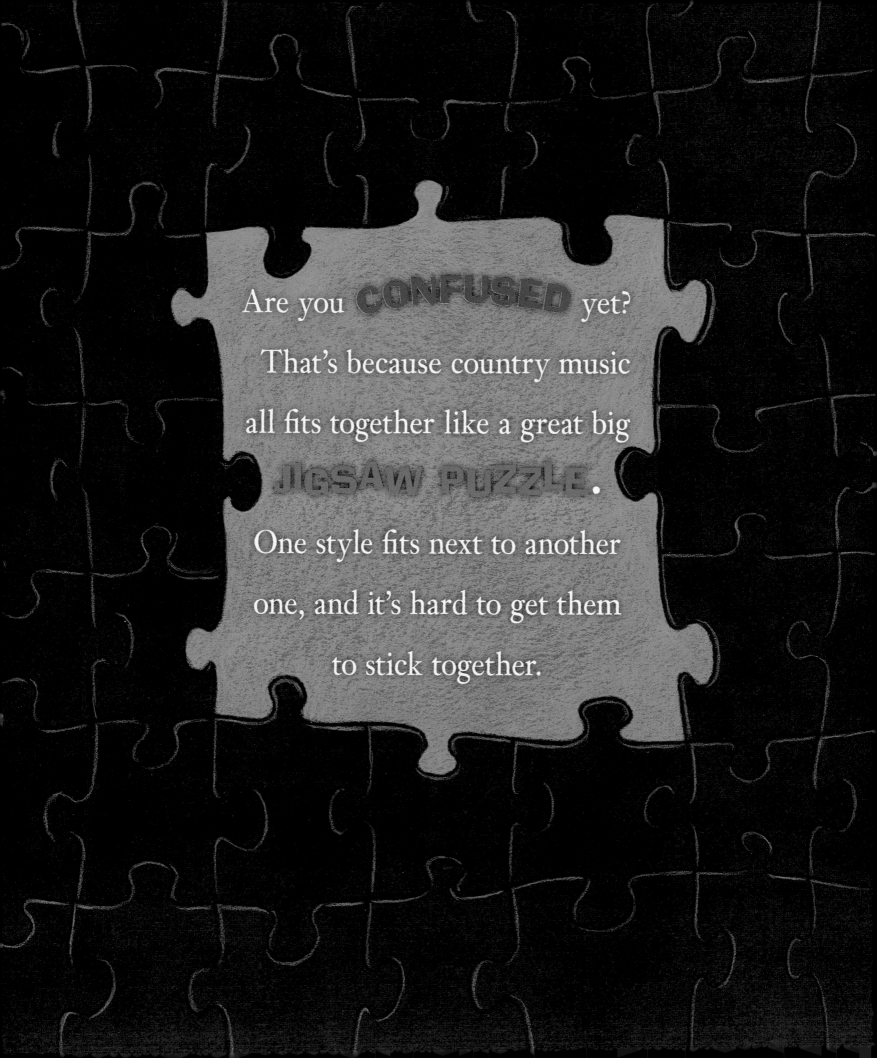

Are you **CONFUSED** yet? That's because country music all fits together like a great big **JIGSAW PUZZLE.**

One style fits next to another one, and it's hard to get them to stick together.

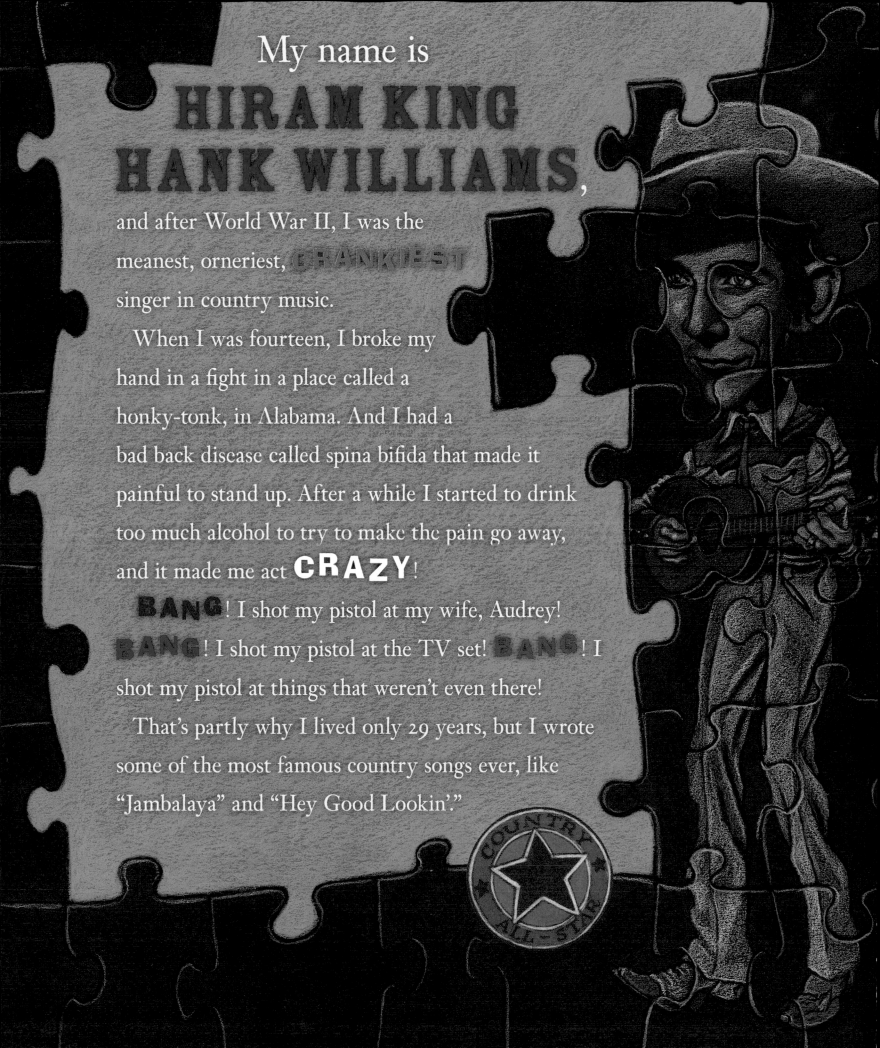

My name is

HIRAM KING HANK WILLIAMS,

and after World War II, I was the meanest, orneriest, CRANKIEST singer in country music.

When I was fourteen, I broke my hand in a fight in a place called a honky-tonk, in Alabama. And I had a bad back disease called spina bifida that made it painful to stand up. After a while I started to drink too much alcohol to try to make the pain go away, and it made me act **CRAZY**!

BANG! I shot my pistol at my wife, Audrey! **BANG**! I shot my pistol at the TV set! **BANG**! I shot my pistol at things that weren't even there!

That's partly why I lived only 29 years, but I wrote some of the most famous country songs ever, like "Jambalaya" and "Hey Good Lookin'."

HONKY·TONKIN'

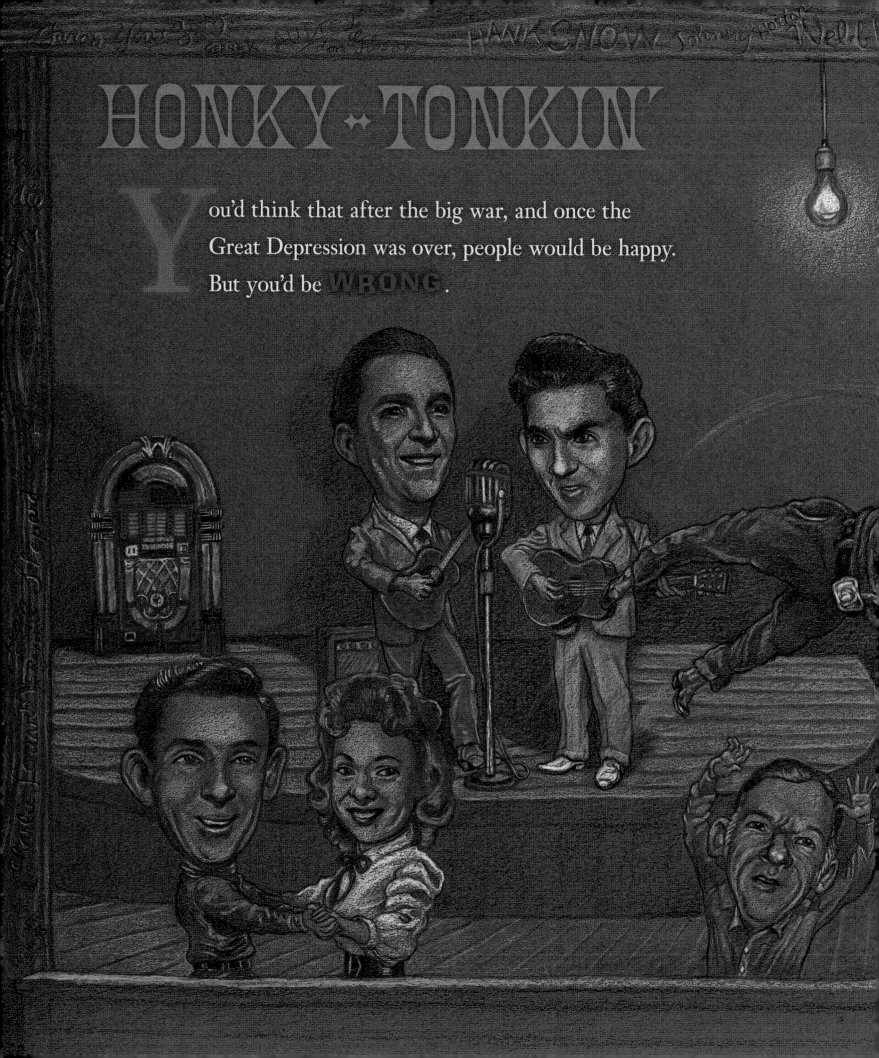

Y ou'd think that after the big war, and once the Great Depression was over, people would be happy. But you'd be WRONG.

Don't let anybody fool you: in the 1950s people were SAD. Maybe too much had happened too fast, or maybe nothing was the same after the war, but you could hear how sad everyone was in the new kind of country music called HONKY TONK. Honky-tonk music was all about being mad or sad. It's called honky-tonk because honky-tonks were places like bars and ROADHOUSES where people went to forget their troubles, drink beer, and dance. Honky-tonk music didn't pretend things were good, but somehow it made you feel better to know that other people felt bad, too.

COUNTRY WORDS

1. **COTTON:** This means you like something, as in, "I sure took a cotton to that chocolate bar."

2. **CRAW:** This is your throat, or that general vicinity. Usually used in a negative sense, as though food were stuck in your throat, like, "That broccoli sticks in my Craw." Can be used for other things like, "Math sticks in my Craw."

craw →

3. **CRICK:** This just means "creek" which is another word for a small river or stream.

4. **DOGGIES:** These aren't dogs; they're cattle.

5. **HANKER:** This means you want something, as in "I HANKER for a hunka cheese."

6. HOLLER: 1. A valley, where country folks live.
   2. To yell at the top of your lungs.

7. 'PRECIATE: Short for "Appreciate." A good way
   to say "thank you."

8. RAT'LER: Short for "rattlesnake."

9. SQUEEZAL: Legendary half squirrel, half weasel.
   Rumored to make a musical sound when squeezed.

10. TWANG: the sound a country guitar makes.
    Also refers to a way of pronouncing words, like "'preciate."

11. Y'ALL: Contraction of "you" and "all." Be sure to use
    this as much as possible, as in, "y'all sure smell funny,"
    or "y'all come back."

Now, try them all together, as in: "Y'all don't 'PRECIATE this TWANG.
That's 'cause you don't eat enough RATLER. I took a COTTON to it
and now I'm HANKERIN' for some. You gotta be careful,
though, or it'll stick in yer CRAW, like 'SQUEEZAL' meat.
Hey, HOLLER at yer friend chasin' DOGGIES down by the CRICK...."

ERASE·ALL

on't get too sad on honky-tonk music!
You can **SLICK BACK YOUR HAIR**, TURN UP YOUR PANT CUFFS, AND GET A TATTOO! 'Cause while all the parents were busy being sad and mad, teenagers started tuning into a new music that scared older people: ROCKABILLY (which is a country word for rock 'n' roll).

Preachers and parents thought it was bad for you, like too much sugar.

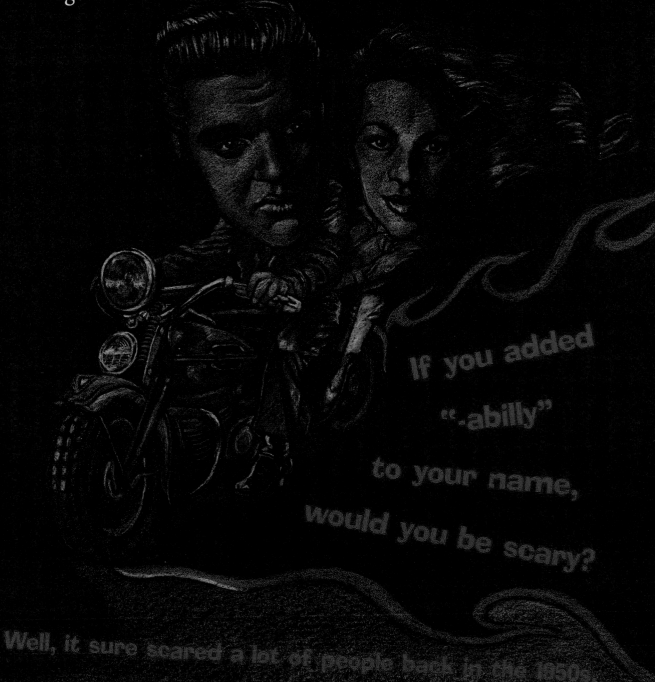

If you added
"-abilly"
to your name,
would you be scary?

Well, it sure scared a lot of people back in the 1950s.

And older country singers were scared most of all because suddenly all the radio stations started to play rockabilly, and soon it was hard to find anyone who wanted to listen to the older style of country music.

COUNTRYPOLITAN

Of course, not **EVERYBODY** wanted to put grease in their hair and listen to music with "-abilly" in it.

By the late 1950s and early 1960s, you could live in a new place called a "**SUBURB**." It wasn't quite country, but it had a lot of space, and it wasn't quite city, but it was "cosmopolitan," (a big word that means "like a city.") Soon, there was music to go with it.

COUNTRY + **COSMOPOLITAN** = **COUNTRYPOLITAN**

It was full of violins, like a city orchestra, and singers in Nashville, like Patsy Cline.

My name is **VIRGINIA HENSLEY**, and I loved Hank Williams's music. After I heard it, I changed my name to **PATSY CLINE** and moved to Nashville, hoping to become a star. But the music people in Nashville thought my voice was too pretty to sing sad honky-tonk songs.

Still, I had a difficult honky-tonk life, traveling all over singing country music, and once I almost died in a car accident. I had a great big scar on my forehead, but I still could **SING**.

Even so, I only recorded music for four years, because I died in a plane crash when I was 30. A lot of country singers died young. I think it's because we lived such weird lives, traveling far away from our families, sometimes for months, and in nasty weather and cheap vehicles.

THE BIG LIST OF COUNTRY NICKNAMES

Nicknames are a great tradition in country music. Think about "Skeeter" Davis or "Stringbean" Akeman or "Homer" & "Jethro." Now YOU can have a country nickname just by using this chart. Find the first letter of your first & last names to get your new country Nickname!

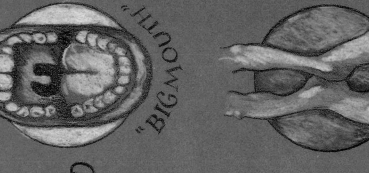

"BIGMOUTH"

"BIGFOOT"

FIRST NAME

A = STINKY
B = GOOBER
C = LEFTY
D = TUBBY
E = COOTER
F = SLIM
G = LITTLE
H = TOOTSIE
I = RED
J = SKEETER

LAST NAME

A = HOGFAT
B = LOUDBOTTOM
C = CHUCKLEHEAD
D = BISCUITS
E = TUMMY
F = GATORFACE
G = SIZZLER
H = TOEJAM
I = BIGMOUTH
J = OUTBACK

"SKEETER"

"BOOTS"

"WIDEPANTS"

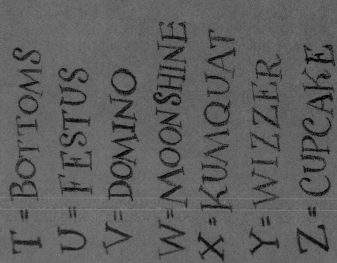

"MOONSHINE"

K = WIDEPANTS
L = BIGFOOT
M = BUCKETS
N = TATER
O = HOWDY
P = CORNCOB
Q = POCKETS
R = STRINGBEAN
S = POOTER
T = BOTTOMS
U = FESTUS
V = DOMINO
W = MOONSHINE
X = KUMQUAT
Y = WIZZER
Z = CUPCAKE

K = BOOTS
L = JUNIOR
M = BOOGER
N = TEX
O = DOC
P = LUCKY
Q = TYLO
R = CRASH
S = KNUCKLES
T = WEENUS
U = TINY
V = POODLE
W = CURLY
X = STUBBY
Y = SHAKE
Z = PANCHO

"KNUCKLES"

"POODLE"

My name is Bill Monroe, and I accidentally started a new kind of country music in the 1930s called **BLUEGRASS**. It was named for the bluegrass of Kentucky, where I was from.

I loved the blues songs my old friend Arnold Schultz taught me, and I learned to play mandolin because my brothers already played guitar and fiddle.

My friends and I used old-time instruments, like the banjo and the big upright bass, to play songs really, really fast. People started to call the way we played "pickin'." I got so fast that the only thing you could pick faster than me was your own **NOSE**! Maybe.

Another thing Americans helped invent after World War II was the TELEVISION. Do you have a **TV**?

Did you know a lot of people didn't have TVs until the **1950s**?

THE AGE OF TV

I calculate it wasn't long before you could see country singers without ever leaving your house.

As far back as 1955, you might have seen parts of the Grand Ole Opry on television.

Stars like Porter Wagoner and Johnny Cash soon had their own shows, too.

By the 1960s and into the '70s country stars turned up regularly on shows like *The Beverly Hillbillies* and *Hee Haw*.

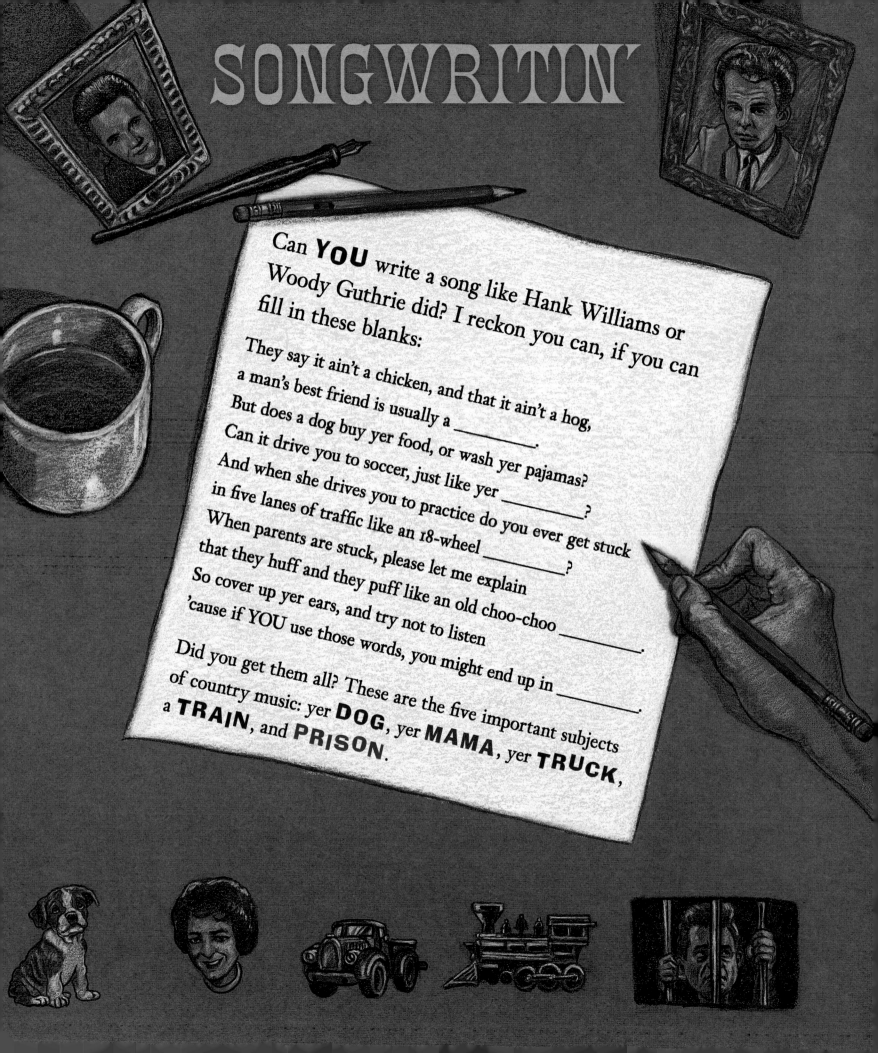

SONGWRITIN'

Can **YOU** write a song like Hank Williams or Woody Guthrie did? I reckon you can, if you can fill in these blanks:

They say it ain't a chicken, and that it ain't a hog,
a man's best friend is usually a _____.
But does a dog buy yer food, or wash yer pajamas?
Can it drive you to soccer, just like yer _____?
And when she drives you to practice do you ever get stuck
in five lanes of traffic like an 18-wheel _____?
When parents are stuck, please let me explain
that they huff and they puff like an old choo-choo _____.
So cover up yer ears, and try not to listen
'cause if YOU use those words, you might end up in _____.

Did you get them all? These are the five important subjects of country music: yer **DOG**, yer **MAMA**, yer **TRUCK**, a **TRAIN**, and **PRISON**.

Heck, I imagine everyone gets in a scuffle now and again, but in the 1970s darn near all of America had something stuck in its craw.

Another stretch of hard times discombob- ulated the country. The war in Vietnam made everyone holler at each other.

And then, just like in the Depression, you had to wait in line for things. People waited for hours to get gas for their cars, like hogs waitin' for slop.

No one liked how anyone else looked,

and people fought about who was a little bit country and who was a little bit rock 'n' roll.

CROSS-OVER

OUTLAW

clean hair

WORN-OUT No HAT HAT

No beard

greasy hair

beard

Leather Vest

Sheer Top-coat

Orange Water Pistol

NO Pistol

Shiny Dress

Blue Jeans

SCUFFED BOOTS

SPARKLE SHOES

Dirty-lookin' performers with long hair and leather clothes were called OUTLAWS. And clean singers, who were "mellow," had big hair, and glitter on their clothes, were called CROSSOVERS, because they had so much money they "crossed over" from country life to city life.

COUNTRY HAIR

In the sixties and seventies,

country music singers had **HAIR** that was **HUGE!**

Maybe it was because they thought the weight of it would smash

down their brains and force out the country music.

Or **MAYBE** it was because the clothes were so spangly and sparkly

they needed huge hair to make it look balanced.

But what's odder than a wig on a chicken is that a lot of men

in country music were **BALD.**

And maybe that's why **THEY** wore great big country **HATS!**

COUNTRY VITTLES!

Some food goes better with country music than others, and probably the most famous country food is **GRITS**! Nobody knows exactly what a "grit" is, but it kinda looks like a pile of sand.

Next is something called **OKRA**, which apparently grows in the South. It might just be a bunch of fried-up flowers, but if you don't make it right, it tastes exactly like a shoe.

Then there's **JAMBALAYA**, which is Cajun for "weird soup." It's the tastiest of all the confounding country edibles, except possibly **GUMBO**. Gumbo is similar to jambalaya, except you never know if it has a crawdad in it or not.

What's a **CRAWDAD**? It's a mythical creature from the South that looks like a tiny lobster. They live near the crick!* (*See "Country Words.")
Finally, there's the greatest country food of all, an **ELVIS SANDWICH**: mashed bananas in peanut butter on fried bread! Yum!

Crystal Gayle & Loretta Lynn

The Judds

Delmore Brothers

Alabama

Statler Brothers

Hank 3

Hank 2

Hank 1

Carter Family

*The answer is the Statler Brothers, none of whom are named "Statler," even though there are two brothers in the group. Only one member of Alabama is not related to the other three cousins.

By the early 1980s, country music had been going along as a big business since 1927. Over FIFTY years! There were people who had kids and cousins and brothers and sisters who also got involved in country music, and they made a big family tree. Can you guess which of these families isn't really a family after all?*

Finally, people got tired of all the fighting. All the country singers worked together in the '70s and '80s because a new kind of music called DISCO had everyone dancing. Once again, it didn't seem like anyone listened to country music.

But when the country people did get together, it was like the formation of a giant

!

By the 1990s, it was unbelievable how many people were singing country music! Men in hats and more women than ever before.

The giant monster could do anything: old styles, rock 'n' roll styles, even disco styles. Anything. It looked like country music might even eat up THE WHOLE DANG WORLD!

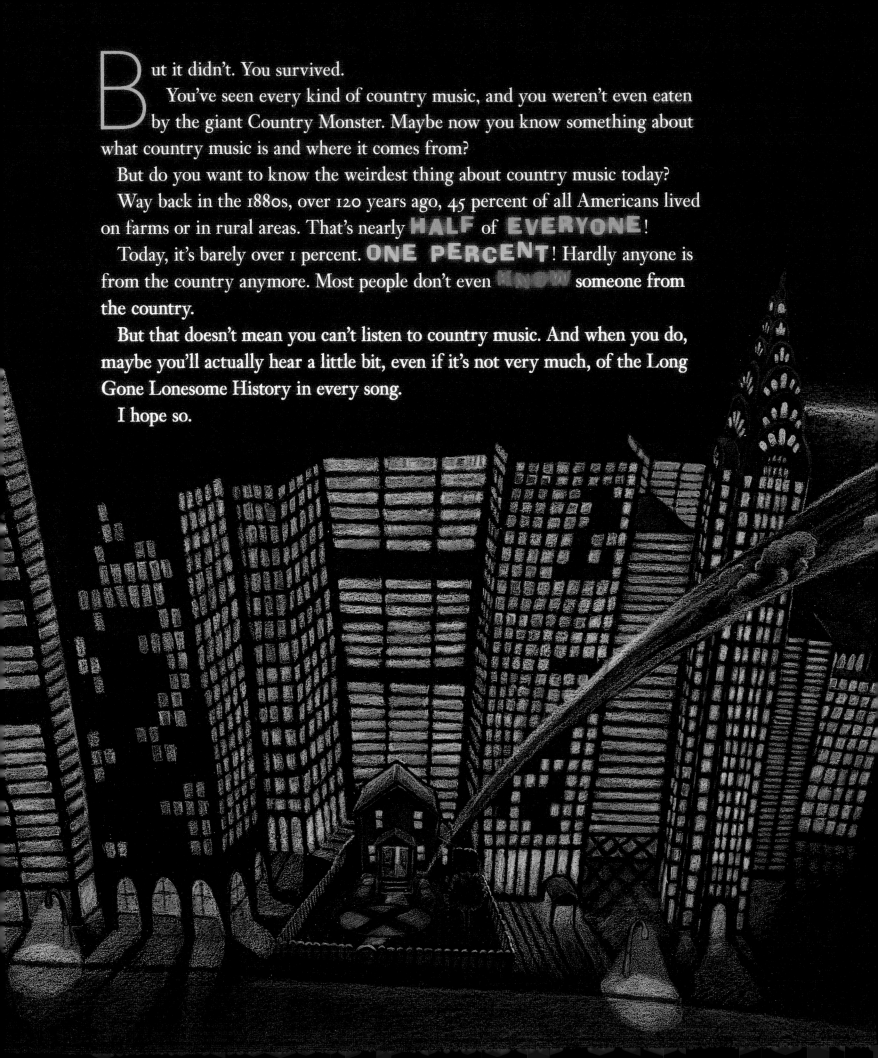

But it didn't. You survived.

You've seen every kind of country music, and you weren't even eaten by the giant Country Monster. Maybe now you know something about what country music is and where it comes from?

But do you want to know the weirdest thing about country music today?

Way back in the 1880s, over 120 years ago, 45 percent of all Americans lived on farms or in rural areas. That's nearly **HALF** of **EVERYONE**!

Today, it's barely over 1 percent. **ONE PERCENT**! Hardly anyone is from the country anymore. Most people don't even **KNOW** someone from the country.

But that doesn't mean you can't listen to country music. And when you do, maybe you'll actually hear a little bit, even if it's not very much, of the Long Gone Lonesome History in every song.

I hope so.

WHO'S WHO in the LONG GONE LONESOME HISTORY:

On the FRONT COVER: (left to right) Jimmie Rodgers; Patsy Cline; Hank Williams, SR; Tammy Wynette; George Jones; Johnny Cash; Charley Pride; and in the sky, Roy Acuff and Ernest Tubb.

On the Opening pages: "tired" is Sleepy LaBeef; "Stinky" is Whitey Ford— the Duke of Paducah; "Lonesome" is Mother Maybelle Carter; "Ugly" is Porter Wagoner (Sorry, MR. Wagoner); "Cranky" is Hank Williams, SR; "Depressed is Moe Bandy; "Silly" is Minnie Pearl; and "Strange" is Uncle Dave Macon.

"WAY DOWN SOUTH": Anonymous musicians from the Appalachian Mountains.

"RADIO DAYS": Lulu Belle & Scotty Wiseman

"EARLY RECORDS": The Carter Family: A.P., Sara, & Maybelle

Behind "JIMMIE RODGERS" is Blind Lemon Jefferson, and behind him is Fiddlin' John Carson.

"The GREAT DEPRESSION": riding in the truck are Huddie LEdbetter (Leadbelly) and Woody Guthrie

"GOSPEL ROOTS": on the left page, top to bottom and left to right: Goebel Reeves; Vernon Dalhart; Emmett Miller; Bradley Kincaid; Roba Stanley; Roscoe Holcomb; Abby Hutchinson; a little girl; and Emma Bell Miles.

On the right page; Charley Patton; Robert Johnson; Son House; Thomas A. Dorsey; Sister Rosetta Tharpe; DeFord Bailey; a little boy; Mahalia Jackson; and Bessie Smith.

"THE SINGING COWBOYS": Gabby Hayes and Gene Autry; Roy Rogers and Dale Evans; Tex Ritter; and in the corner, Tex Williams,

"So Let's Get Dressed": Little Jimmy Dickens and Tanya Tucker.

"Hillbilly Jazz": in the bowl, clockwise from the top: Louis Armstrong; José Alfredo Jiménez; Milton Brown; Bix Beiderbecke; W.C. Handy; Duke Ellington; and Pee Wee King.

"WORLD WAR II": dancing are Patti Page and Jimmy Wakely; Ernest Tubb is on the poster; Gene Autry is writing to his mom.

"NASHVILLE": onstage are Jake Tullock; Roy Acuff; and Ernest Tubb.

"HONKY TONKIN'": from the left: Ray Price dancing with Jean Shepard; Faron Young; Webb Pierce; Lefty Frizzell leaping; Hank Snow ducking; Johnny Horton losing his hair, Goldie Hill; & Kitty Wells.

"ROCK A BILLY": Elvis Presley; Wanda Jackson; Johnny Cash; Billy Graham (with stop sign); Jerry Lee Lewis; Buddy Holly; Don & Phil Everly; Red Foley (holding sign)

"COUNTRYPOLITAN": Skeeter Davis; Jim Reeves; Chet Atkins.

"FIVE RULES OF BLUEGRASS": left to right: Lester Flatt; Earl Scruggs; Carter & Ralph Stanley; Hazel Dickens.

"TELEVISION": Minnie Pearl; John F. Kennedy; the Beverly Hillbillies; Martin Luther King; Buck Owens & Roy Clark on HEE HAW; the "General Lee."

"SONGWRITIN'": upper left is Roger Miller; upper right is Merle Haggard; below are Mother Maybelle Carter and Johnny Cash

"HARD TIMES & BAD HAIR": (Top to bottom, left to right) George Jones; Jerry Reed; Merle Haggard; Bob Dylan; Conway Twitty; Gram Parsons; Kris Kristofferson; John Denver; Marie Osmond; Willie Nelson; Olivia Newton-John; Waylon Jennings.

"COUNTRY HAIR": Garth Brooks; Loretta Lynn; Dolly Parton; Tammy Wynette; Hank Williams, SR.

"BEWARE! (THE COUNTRY MONSTER)": (left to right) Faith Hill; Shania Twain; Alan Jackson; Vince Gill; Garth Brooks; George Strait; and Reba McEntire.

In the rocket ship are Wayne Hancock; Gillian Welch & Dwight Yoakam; ON the BACK COVER are Willie Nelson; Patsy Montana; Loretta Lynn; Marty Robbins & Eddy Arnold.